Treasure of All Treasures

An Eternal Inheritance

Amanda Delahoussaye

Copyright © 2017

Amanda Delahoussaye

All Rights Reserved.

ISBN: 13: 978-1978377387

Scriptures marked AMP are taken from the AMPLIFIED BIBLE (AMP): Scripture taken from the AMPLIFIED® BIBLE, Copyright © 1954, 1958, 1962, 1964, 1965, 1987 by the Lockman Foundation Used by Permission.

Scriptures marked NIV are taken from the NEW INTERNATIONAL VERSION (NIV): Scripture taken from THE HOLY BIBLE, NEW INTERNATIONAL VERSION ®. Copyright©1973, 1978, 1984, 2011 by Biblica, Inc.™. Used by permission of Zondervan

Scriptures marked NKJV are taken from the NEW KING JAMES VERSION (NKJV): Scripture taken from the NEW KING JAMES VERSION®. Copyright© 1982 by Thomas Nelson, Inc.Used by permission. All rights reserved.

Scripture quotations taken from the New American Standard Bible® (NASB), Copyright © 1960.1962,1963,1968,1971,1972,1973,1975,1977,1995 by The Lockman Foundation Used by permission.

All Greek and Hebrew words are italicized. They are taken from The New Strong's Exhaustive Concordance Of The Bible, James Strong, 1990 copyright© by Thomas Nelson Publishers.

Acknowledgments

I want to thank my Lord and Savior, Jesus Christ, first and foremost for His Presence in my life. He is the priceless Treasure which has made my life worth living.

Thank you, Rebecca LaFleur, Jeff and Sue Murton and Dino Griffin for your reviews.

Thank you, Gloria Breaux, for your input in the editing process.

Bethany Sugg, I appreciate your technical input.

Graphic Design by Maygan Montz

CONTENTS

Dedication………………………………… 8

Foreword by Jeff Murton, Dino Griffin,
And Rebecca LaFleur…………………... 14

Teaching

Chapter 1	His Resting Place………..	18
Chapter 2	What About Faith?……….	31
Chapter 3	Faith Works Through Love………………………	43

Personal Life Lessons

Chapter 4	My Journey Begins...........	51
Chapter 5	The Candlestick...............	59
Chapter 6	Ten Virgins....................	89
Chapter 7	Revival Outpouring...........	95
Chapter 8	The Sunflower................	98
Chapter 9	Strength in Our Weakness......................	109
Chapter 10	Through the Fire..............	112
Chapter 11	Peace Only He Gives..........	116
Chapter 12	Focus............................	120
Chapter 13	Drawing Near..................	124
Chapter 14	Grieving the Heart Of God.........................	147

Chapter 15	Our Worth………………	152
Chapter 16	Mirror Mirror …………..	158
Chapter 17	The Mandate……………	165
Chapter 18	The Blessing……………..	170

Dedication

The Lord, in-spite of me, by the unction of His Spirit directed this book. All glory is His!

Joel 1:3

Tell your children about it, and let your children tell their children, and their children the next generation.

In Joel, the Lord instructs parents to teach their children the Word and ways of God. I endeavor to do that in writing this book.

This book is based on a vision the Lord gave to me when I was 17 years old. The simplistic style is intended to appeal to a broad range of readers, written as though I am telling my story at the kitchen table.

This book is dedicated to my children: Maria and David, Leah and Andrew, Bethany and Thomas, to my grandchildren: Dylan, Alyssa, Jacob, Noah and to my future grandchildren for a thousand generations to come as they are my treasures from heaven.

It is dedicated to all those who are wise, those who thirst, those who hunger, those who are desperate and know it, those who recognize the void deep in the core of their being, those who are willing, and to those who are of a humble and contrite heart.

Psalm 37:18

The Lord knows the days of the upright, and their inheritance shall be forever.

A legacy is something you impart to others and an inheritance is something you leave for others.

To my children and my grandchildren to a thousand generations, I desire to impart a legacy that will impact their lives for eternity and leave an inheritance that will change the world around them.

Psalm 105:8
He remembers His covenant forever, the word which He commanded for a thousand generations

Exodus 20: 6
But showing mercy and steadfast love to a thousand generations of those who love Me and keep My commandments.

Isaiah 54:13
All your children shall be taught by the Lord, and great shall be the peace of your children.

Isaiah 49:25
...For I will contend with him who contends with you, And I will save your children.

As children of God, we are promised in the covenant the Lord has made with us that His mercy and love would be passed down to our children and our children's children up to a thousand generations. He will teach our children and great will be their peace. I believe and stand on the promise of God to save and teach my children.

Acts 3:6

Then Peter said, "Silver and gold I do not have, but what I do have I give you…"

As I grow older, I often think of the one thing I would most want to leave my children and grandchildren for an inheritance. This one thing is more precious than gold, silver, or diamonds and once you experience Him, nothing else compares. He is the most precious of all treasures—*Treasure of all Treasures*.

At the church I attend, we sing a song in worship by a group called Lamb with the Hebrew word *Tshalach* in it. The word "*Tshalach*" means to, 'send forth Your Spirit' or to 'break out mightily Your Spirit.'

I pray *Tshalach* to you as you read the words of these pages. The Lord send forth His Spirit upon you and breakout mightily His Spirit in your life.

John 6:35

And Jesus said to them, "I am the Bread of Life. He who comes to Me shall never hunger, and he who believes in Me shall never thirst."

Within these pages, I serve you Jesus, the Bread of Life, which gives another meaning to the phrase we say often as Christians, "I serve the Lord." Just as my sweet mother-in-law taught me at her kitchen table, a good host serves the best to satisfy the guest. I give you the best; I serve you Jesus, the Bread of Life, which will satisfy and yet you will hunger for more.

Foreword

As soon as we met Amanda at a group ministry meeting in Lafayette a number of years ago, it was obvious to us that she had an intimate and powerful relationship with Jesus. Since then, it has been our pleasure to spend time with Amanda and her husband at their home, and minister together with her.

Through "Treasure of All Treasures," Amanda brings some powerful teaching from God's Word on understanding the privilege and power of salvation in Jesus and the indwelling Holy Spirit. Through God's revelation to her she unpacks deep insights into the Menorah and the

Tabernacle, and brings out gems of life through a number of different life lessons.

This book will take you deeper into the heart of God for your own life, unlock the Beauty of intimacy, and challenge you to know Jesus as the true, Treasure Of All Treasures.

Thanks, Amanda, for this legacy.

Rev. Jeff Murton

There are times in life when you connect with someone who will forever be a kindred spirit. That connection for me was made when I met Amanda Delahoussaye. She opens her heart and soul to become transparent, believing others can leave their past behind, be forgiven, and reach for a greater intimacy with the Lord to fulfill their calling.

God can take broken lives, broken hearts, and create brand new lives and give brand new hearts for His Glory. Jesus paid the ultimate price with His own life, paying a debt He did not owe for a debt we could not pay. After reading this book you will know you were worth fighting and dying for.

This book reminds me of God's power to love and reach anyone no matter where you are and what you've done, so that your true purpose can be fulfilled. Then, you will be able to leave your own legacy of hope.

Evangelist Rebecca LaFleur
Jesus is Lord Ministries

Amanda,

Thank you for the privilege of reading your manuscript. Your added antidotes made everything more personal and helped to draw me into the great story of God's redeeming love for us.

I like the simplicity of your writing, your generous usage of the Scriptures, and felt like you were simply telling your story. Many books I have read that attempt to convey what you have written come across as preachy and impassive. But your manuscript betrays a deep humility, a powerful passion for Jesus, and a compassionate appeal to your audience.

You did a good job expressing a biblically sound, clear and attractive presentation of the Gospel.

Under His Mercy,

Pastor Dino Griffin

CHAPTER 1

His Resting Place

Isaiah 66: 1-2

Thus says the Lord: "Heaven is My throne, and earth is My footstool. Where is the house that you will build Me? And where is the place of My rest? For all those things My hand has made, and all those things exist," says the Lord. "But on this one will I look: On him who is humble and of a contrite spirit, and who trembles at My word.

With all of heaven as His throne and the earth as His footstool, He still yet desires to rest, to inhabit, and to dwell in and among man whom He created. The man who is poor in spirit is one who is humble in spirit, repentant of sin, and trembles at His word. He is one who is in awe of the majesty and purity of God and His word. Such a heart is one that is a living temple for the Lord. The Lord favors this heart with His holy Presence; it is the chosen place of His rest.

Genesis 1:26 & 27 says in the beginning God created man in His image. God breathed or imparted His breath into man. We were to subdue the earth and have dominion over the earth. We were God's image bearers. Man had unbroken communion with God and walked with God.

Genesis 2:18

And the Lord God said, "It is not good that man should be alone; I will make him a helper comparable to him."

Everything God does, He does on purpose and with a purpose. He does nothing nonchalantly. Even in creating Eve after He created Adam, God had a purpose. He created us with the need for human companionship and Adam was no different. Spiritually, Adam was completely fulfilled by and in God before the fall.

It was not a surprised for our Creator to see it wasn't good for Adam to be alone. It was not the Lord's intention for Adam to dwell on the earth alone.

In creating Eve, Adam's need for human companionship would be met. Eve was to help alleviate Adam's aloneness, as well as, he hers.

In understanding his (Adam's) own yearning for a loving relationship and intimacy with someone of his likeness, he would understand God's yearning for a loving relationship with mankind. God said, "*It is not good for man to be alone.*" This longing for companionship and intimacy with someone of our likeness is created in us. It is a Godlike trait. It is the same longing God has for a relationship, companionship, and intimacy with someone of His likeness, which is man. It's the motive of the heart of God in creating man. Without this desire, we wouldn't know or understand His longing for a loving relationship with us.

God is love and love has to have an object to express itself to. God being love, He created you and me as the object to express His great love to and through. The Lord has emotions. He feels love, joy, peace, anger, and He can be grieved. As a matter of fact, He dances over us with exuberant joy and singing (Zephaniah 3:17). Because we are created in the image of God, Adam had a God given need to express love— then there was woman!

After the fall of man, we were separated from His Presence, no longer intimately communing with Him. Sin, death and separation from the Presence of God changed man and the earth from God's original order. But, God had His plan to restore His resting place in man's heart and life.

John 1: 1-5

In the beginning was the Word, and the Word was with God, and the Word was God. He was in the beginning with God. All things were made through Him, and without Him nothing was made that was made. In Him was life, and the life was the light of men. And the light shines in the darkness, and the darkness did not comprehend it.

John 1: 14

And the Word became flesh and dwelt among us, and we beheld His glory, the glory as of the only begotten of the Father, full of grace and truth.

John 3:16

For God so loved the world that He gave His only begotten Son, that whoever believes in Him should not perish but have everlasting life.

Ephesians 2:13

But now in Christ Jesus you who once were far off have been brought near by the blood of Christ.

God presented Jesus as the sacrifice for atonement or reconciliation with mankind.

Fellowship with our Father could only be realized or restored through atoning for the sins that separated mankind from Him and His promises. It is the shed blood of Christ that ultimately satisfied the requirements of God's justice. God's judgment was fully put upon Christ, the blameless sacrifice, for all our sins past, present and future.

It is through faith in the blood of Christ that man is justified and restored into His Presence. The blood of Jesus Christ is forever the only means of a right relationship with His holy Presence.

2 Corinthians 4:7

But we have this treasure in earthen vessels, that the excellence of the power may be of God and not of us.

Jesus made the way for our hearts and lives to be the dwelling place of His Presence once again. Jesus, through the cross, ripped the curtain of division between man and His holy Presence. There is no longer a separation between God and His people. Through Jesus we are His dwelling place. We now have access or privilege of entry into this Holy Place if we so choose.

1 John 4:17

Love has been perfected among us in this: that we may have boldness in the Day of Judgment; because as He is, so are we in this world.

In the work of the Cross, Jesus didn't only take our place as our sacrifice; He also placed us seated with Him in heavenly places. In other words, today we can have our residence with Him in His seat of authority. As He is, so are we in this world. Jesus took our place on the cross as our sacrifice to give us all the benefits of who He is.

Proverbs 21:20

There is a desirable treasure, and oil in the dwelling of the wise, but a foolish man squanders it.

Desirable treasure is a beautiful, delightful deposit which refers to the wealth of God's Holy Presence, the *Treasure of All Treasures*. It is coveted and extremely valued. True riches are found in His Presence and in knowing Him intimately. With Jesus, the impossible, the too difficult, and the unbelievable become possible.

Oil refers to the Presence of God. Those who are wise know the value of the oil of His Presence and do not squander it. "Cherish" means 'to treasure, adore and value.' The wise cherish the impartation of His Presence through intimately knowing Him. Intimacy with Jesus is the key to the oil of His Presence and sustaining it. The wise know the cost of this Treasure, the high and costly price of the death of God's Son. They are willing to pay the price to know Him because His Presence is highly valued. The wise handle His Presence with care, fear and trembling and do not squander it.

"Squander" is defined as, 'to waste, to thoughtlessly allow to pass, or to be lost.' The wise do not allow the opportunity of housing His Presence to thoughtlessly pass, to be lost or to be wasted.

The greater the measure of His Presence the greater the responsibility we have not to waste or squander it. We must recognize our moment of visitation as to not squander it.

When you find this Treasure, know that it is always for a purpose. He doesn't come into our life for the sole purpose of making us look good or feel good. His Presence is for the purpose of use, not only in our own life but also in the lives of those around us. It is to be cherished, nurtured and given away. We receive freely and we must give freely.

In *Matthew 25: 1-13* Jesus gives the parable of 10 Virgins. The foolish virgins squandered their oil while the wise virgins desired and valued the oil above all else. They delighted in the treasure of oil they possessed understanding the value of it and the price that was paid for the privilege of possessing it. The wise virgins took special care of and gave attention to the oil they possessed. They were willing to do what they had to do to maintain the oil in their lives.

Maintaining intimacy with Him and growing in the wisdom of the knowledge of God is essential to maintaining the precious oil of the Holy Spirit. We pay a high price when we squander the oil, because He paid the ultimate price for us to enjoy the privilege of it. The foolish virgins came to Jesus and begged for the door to be opened. Jesus said, *"Truly I tell you, I don't know you."* The door was shut with no way in.

Job 22: 21

Now acquaint yourself with Him, and be at peace; thereby good will come to you.

"Acquaint" means 'to agree with God and show yourself to be conformed to His will.' We cannot agree with Him unless we know Him. That word "*good*" in the Hebrew means, 'good in the widest sense of the word, all things good; prosperity, peace, wealth, joy, victory, and favor.'

The Amplified Bible says it this way: *Acquaint now yourself with Him (agree with God and show yourself to be conformed to His will) and be at peace; by that (you shall prosper and great) good shall come to you.*

Wow! In just knowing Him we have the *Treasure of All Treasures*, but He goes far above in as much as giving us great good and prosperity as we align our lives with His will. It is our Father's good pleasure to give us, His children, the Kingdom.

CHAPTER 2

What About Faith?

Hebrews 11:6

But without faith it is impossible to please Him, for he who comes to God must believe that He is, and that He is a rewarder of those who diligently seek Him.

Romans 12:3

For I say, through the grace given to me, to everyone who is among you, not to think of himself more highly than he ought to think, but to think soberly, as God has dealt to each one a measure of faith.

The word "dealt" means 'to give or to bestow a portion or a share.' God has bestowed or given to each one of us a measure or a limited portion of faith. Hebrews 11:6 states that it is impossible to please God without faith. God Himself has given to each one of us the faith it takes to please Him or the faith it takes to choose Him. Our responsibility is to use the faith He has given and make the decision to choose Him. He will not make that choice for us. It must be a deliberate act of our will to choose and love Him; otherwise, it wouldn't be love.

John 6:44

"No one can come to Me unless the Father who sent Me draws him; and I will raise him up at the last day."

No one can come to Jesus unless he is first drawn by the Father. God has given us what we need to please Him. He has given us faith and He does the drawing. We make the decision; That, He will not do for us.

Deuteronomy 30:19-20

I call heaven and earth as witnesses today against you, that I have set before you life and death, blessing and cursing: therefore choose life that both you and your descendants may live. That you may love the Lord your God that you may obey His voice, and that you may cling to Him, for He is your life and the length of your days, and that you may dwell in the land which the Lord swore to your fathers...

He has made it very simple for us. All we have to do is choose Jesus, cling to Him and live. When He draws us, we have a choice, either to use the faith He has given us to respond to Him or not. He has supplied it all for us. We have no excuse; man is without excuse.

Matthew 17:20

"...if you have faith as a mustard seed, you will say to this mountain, move from here to there and it will move, and nothing will be impossible for you."

The size of a mustard seed is not big. It's a tiny speck of a seed and that's all it takes. This faith He has portioned to each one of us grows by hearing the word and renewing our hearts and minds with the Word.

Romans 10:17

So then faith comes by hearing, and hearing by the word of God.

It is our responsibility to hear the word of God daily in order for that mustard seed of faith to grow. Jesus is the Word of God and our Daily Bread therefore we must choose Him daily in order to nurture and increase our faith.

Matthew 14:30-33

But when he (Peter) saw that the wind was boisterous, he was afraid, and beginning to sink he cried out, saying, "Lord, save me!" And immediately Jesus stretched out His hand and caught him, and said to him, "O you of little faith, why did you doubt?" And when they got into the boat, the wind ceased. Then those who were in the boat came and worshiped Him saying, "Truly You are the Son of God."

Peter began to fear and doubt when he was on the water because of the storm. He was faced with a decision in the midst of the storm. He had life and death before him. Fear and doubt were coming against his mind because his eyes were on the storm. Faith does not come from the mind; it comes from the heart. A renewed mind enhances our faith through an understanding of the unseen.

Peter chose life by choosing to use the faith he had inside and direct that faith towards Jesus. He cried out to Jesus to save him in the midst of fear and doubt. Jesus saved Peter, because Peter chose to put his faith in Jesus in spite of the fact he was sinking. Because we experience fear and doubt, doesn't indicate we have no faith.

In the midst of fear and doubt, we all still have that measure of faith within that God has dealt to us. We can choose to use it and direct it towards Jesus just as Peter did, or we can choose not to.

Fear and doubt are no match for the faith of God, for the power of God or for the grace of God. God has given us everything we need to live in Him and be victorious in Him.

Jesus heard the cry of faith in the midst of the fear and doubt Peter was experiencing. Even though all Peter felt was fear and doubt, he chose by an act of his will to go against his feelings and cry out to Jesus to save him. Faith is not a feeling; it is the power to choose life in Jesus. Jesus responded to that measure of faith Peter was using and reached out and saved Peter from sinking. He put him back in the boat and calmed the storm.

When Jesus asked Peter to get out of the boat and walk on the water, He was saying, walk on the water **with** Me. He was saying, I will be on the water **with** you and if you should sink, I will be here to catch you, to save you and to rescue you. When you take that step of faith to obey God in the midst of a storm, Jesus will be with you in the storm and on the water. Don't worry about sinking; but if you do, call on Jesus and He will be there to save you. Too many of us don't walk on the water because we are afraid of sinking, but with Jesus, it's a win-win situation; we can't lose.

In the midst of our storms in life when fear and doubt are all we feel, we too can use the measure of faith dealt to us to cry out to Jesus despite the way we feel or what we see. His arm is not too short that He cannot save. Whosoever calls on the name of the Lord will be saved even in the midst of fear and doubt. It is easy to have faith in the absence of fear and doubt when circumstances are peaceful. Actually, it doesn't take much faith in those circumstances. The strength of our faith is tested in the circumstances where fear and doubt are all we experience. Faith is choosing life in Jesus in spite of what we feel.

Jesus Himself in the garden of Gethsemane was under such emotional distress that He was sweating drops of blood. To get to such a state, you have to be under extreme stress. In spite of the turmoil He was in, He cried out to His Father and received strength to endure the horrendous suffering and death on the cross for our salvation.

There are times the Lord will allow us to enter into desperate situations so we will cry out to Him, and then, He will show us He is able and willing. The essence of faith or the most important feature of faith is seeking Him and getting to know Him in all circumstances, not just the feel good situations.

When Jesus pulled Peter out of the water and asked him why he doubted, Jesus did not say he had no faith. He told Peter he had little faith. The mustard seed of faith was all it took for Jesus to save Peter. Jesus did not condemn Peter for little faith; however, He was making Peter aware that he needed to allow his faith to grow in order to walk on the water with Jesus.

All we need is a tiny speck of faith to get us through a whole lot of turmoil. If fear and doubt stopped the hand of God and the power of God, Jesus wouldn't have reached out to save Peter. How many people in the Word of God, when they were in situations where God did the miraculous, did not fear or doubt at some point?

As a matter of fact, human nature cries out to God when faced with trouble. This is the measure of faith God dealt to each one of us. Men in prison, soldiers in war, and people in accidents all call out to God. Even atheists have been known to call on God when they are terrified. We frown upon those kinds of last resort prayers. The other option is choosing not to call out at all, therefore, choosing death which is the ultimate display of pride and rebellion. Choose life, Cry Out to Jesus!

Hebrews 12:2

Looking unto Jesus, the author and finisher of our faith, who for the joy that was set before Him endured the cross, despising the shame, and has sat down at the right hand of the throne of God.

The word "looking" in this verse means, 'looking away from all distractions and setting our eyes on Jesus.' Our responsibility is to set our eyes on Jesus no matter the fear, doubt or circumstances we face. The word "author" is defined as, 'the person who originated or gave existence to anything and whose authorship determines responsibility for what was created.'

In other words, our responsibility is to look to Jesus, who is the originator, or the One who gave existence to our faith and the One who takes responsibility for finishing our faith.

Jesus has done it all for us; He has made it simple for us. All we have to do is choose life by choosing Him.

Jesus is the originator of His plan of salvation, and He is also the one who finished it on Calvary. The word "finisher" means, 'one that has been fattened and ready for slaughter.' Jesus is the Lamb of God who was slain before the foundations of the world for you and me as a fattened Lamb without blemish. He will finish what He started in us as we choose Him daily and in all circumstances.

In Luke 22:32, Jesus prayed that Peter's faith would not fail. I also pray that our faith would not fail and grow exponentially.

CHAPTER 3

Faith Works Through Love

Galatians 5:6

For in Christ Jesus neither circumcision nor uncircumcision avails anything but faith working through love.

The word "through" is defined as, 'the channel of an act' and also 'because of.' Therefore, love is the channel by which faith operates, and faith works as a result of love. You cannot have faith absent of the love of God. The love of God is paramount to our existence in Christ. It is the source of our faith.

His love is what compelled Him to deal to each one of us a measure of faith thereby we are able to please Him. (Hebrews 11:6)

Love wouldn't be love if it were forced upon us. The purpose for free will is that we would willingly choose Him as an act of love and faith. It could be said that *free will* is an essential component of love.

The Amplified Bible says it this way:

For in Christ Jesus, neither circumcision nor uncircumcision counts for anything but only faith activated and energized and expressed and working through love. (Galatians 5:6)

When we get a revelation of the Love of God, it is the fuel to our faith as well as being the expression of our faith.

I Corinthians 13:2

And though I have the gift of prophecy and understand all mysteries and all knowledge, and though I have all faith, so that I could remove mountains, but have not love, I am nothing.

I Corinthians 13:7-8

(Love) bears all things, believes all things, hopes all things, endures all things. Love never fails…

The Love of God ignites our faith to believe all things in God and hope all things in God. It's not about our love for Him; it's about His love for us. Experiencing and knowing His love is when faith explodes in our hearts. We can't depend on our love for Him because ours is fickle; here one day and gone the next. His love never fails and His love is perfect. I like to say it this way: He loves us perfectly! Perfect love casts out fear, doubt and unbelief. (1 John 4:18)

Relationship with our loving Father is key in overcoming fear, doubt and unbelief. We were created to rule with Christ through intimacy with Him, which brings forth the Light of God, and that Light is what eradicates darkness.

1Corinthians 13:13

And now abide faith, hope, love, these three: but the greatest of these is love.

We cannot know or have true faith and hope in God without knowing the love of God. This is why the love of God is greatest. Faith and hope are characteristics of the love of God.

As the love of God is revealed to us, our "no" is turned into "yes," our doubt turns into faith and our fear turns into peace. This is the love He wants to communicate to us and through us.

Revelation of the Love of God enables us to love and trust Christ boundlessly with no limits, thereby, faith operates. It would be fitting for us to do as the Apostle Paul instructed us to do, "pursue the love as revealed in Christ Jesus."

Romans 8: 38-39

For I am persuaded that neither death, nor life, nor angels, nor principalities, nor powers, nor things present, nor things to come, nor height nor depth, nor any other created thing, shall be able to separate us from the love of God which is in Christ Jesus our Lord.

One night, I was just about to fall asleep and the Lord spoke to me and asked me a question. He said, "What was it that motivated Me to allow Myself to be beaten beyond recognition and give Myself to be nailed to the cross?" Then He said, "I want you to see yourself as the one who beat Me and nailed Me to the cross." I realize the reason He asked me to ponder this was because it wasn't just some Roman soldier who crucified Jesus. It was my sin that sent Him to the cross. It was just as if I was the one driving the nails in His hands and feet. He said, "I want you to see yourself crucifying Me, and while crucifying Me, I want you to know it is My love for you that drove me to the cross. Know that My love for the very one that has crucified Me is the reason I gave My life. See that I have given My life for the one whose sin drove the nails in my hands and feet."

In my mind, I had envisioned soldier figures beating Him and crucifying Him. But then, I realized it was me through my sin that crucified Him. While He was going through the torture I had caused Him, He had me on His mind saying, "Father, forgive her, for she knows not what she does." Though our sin was the cause,

His love for you and me is what drove Him to the cross.

While we were still in our sin, He died for us. Before we give our life to Jesus and accept His blood sacrifice for the cleansing of our sin, the very nature of sin causes us to be at enmity with God. It causes us to be enemies of God, not by the will of God, but by the nature of sin. We can say it this way, while we were yet an enemy of His, Christ died for us. Scarcely does one give his life for a friend; but to die for an enemy! What Love!

1 John 4:18

There is no fear in love; but perfect love casts out fear, because fear involves torment. But he who fears has not been made perfect in love.

Doubt and torment are characteristics of fear. His love obliterates and exterminates fear from our hearts. If you have fear, seek to know Him for He is love. God has not given us the spirit of fear, but of love, power and a sound mind. (2 Timothy 1:7)

Ephesians 3:19

To know the love of Christ which passes knowledge; that you may be filled with all the fullness of God.

With every revelation of the love of God, we are more filled with the faith of God. Knowing the depth, width and height of His love produces the fullness of God in us.

CHAPTER 4

My Journey Begins

I am a simple Cajun woman born and raised in Louisiana. Seventh of ten children-- talk about middle child syndrome! Born with a rare astigmatism, I had to begin to wear very thick, coke bottle looking glasses in first grade. Since I can remember, I was always a chubby child and struggled with my weight throughout my life. As a teenager, I began to have severe scarring acne. If you can picture a chubby, short kid, with thick coke bottle glasses and cystic acne then you have a pretty good idea of what I looked like when I was a teenager. Always ridiculed and with few friends, I felt like an ugly duckling with a seriously damaged self-image.

Although I wasn't raised in a religious home, Jesus encountered me at a young age. My very first encounter with the Presence of the Lord, in retrospect, happened when I was about eight years old. I was sitting in the living room of our home in front of the television. With no one else watching it at the time, it happened to be on a religious program. The preacher was talking about Jesus and how He loves us. All of a sudden, I noticed tears rolling from my eyes down my cheeks. I didn't understand why I was crying. The preacher had said right at that moment that there was someone watching with tears rolling down your cheeks.

He said, "That is the Lord touching your heart." At the time, I did not understand what to do with that, but looking back I know the Lord had His hand on my life before I even knew Him.

At fourteen years of age, one night, I went to lie on my bed and suddenly I began to feel very afraid and anxious. At the same time, I instantly began to feel an insatiable void and an urgent need for God in my life. I jumped up from my bed, went to my mom's bedroom where she was sleeping and began to cry while pounding my fist on her bed insisting that I needed God in my life. No one in my family knew very much about the Lord at that time and we were not church-goers when I was growing up. Needless to say, she didn't know what to do with this confused and fearful teenager waking her in the middle of the night and vehemently insisting that I needed God in my life.

My mom replied by saying, "Well honey, maybe God has something special for you." Later, I realized, He has something special for all of us and He is eager to give His kingdom to His children.

I had no idea how to process what was going on with me nor did I understand this desperate feeling I suddenly had for God in my life. I knew no one who could help me understand what was going on. I did the only thing I knew to do which was to go talk to a priest. He prayed with me and sent me on my way. Unsure, empty and knowing there had to be more to what I was experiencing, I began trying to live my life as normal as possible.

Still searching, hungry for God, and not knowing how to fill this void in my soul, at the age of fifteen, I became pregnant and married a childhood friend. It was after we married, just before I was to turn sixteen, I had my first child on Christmas day of 1979. Even though it was a joyful time, I couldn't shake this desperate need for God.

As I was home with my first born, I was flipping through the channels on the television. I came to a channel that I was not familiar with. A man was talking about God and how to be saved or born again. Although I didn't understand what the terms "saved" or "born again" meant, I knew in my heart this was what I needed to do to begin to satisfy this void I had deep in my soul.

The man on television began leading the prayer of salvation, and I followed along with him accepting Jesus Christ into my heart and life at the age of sixteen.

John 3:3

Jesus answered and said to him, "Most assuredly, I say to you, unless one is born again, he cannot see the kingdom of God."

This was the beginning of my journey of intimacy with my Creator. It was the beginning of getting to know the One who gave His life for me. I made the choice to use the faith He gave me and I chose Jesus.

This was the first impartation of His Presence in my life. In John 14:6 Jesus said, "*No one can come to the Father except through Me*." Jesus is the way to the Father. If you know Jesus you know and see the Father. As I said, this was only the beginning. The Lord had so much more for me in His Presence; a lifetime of treasures to enjoy and share.

Soon after that, I started going to a church that began to teach me about this new life in Christ. Not long after attending this church, I knew the Lord had more for me. I was taught about intimately knowing God and going deeper into the ways of God. I began learning about the baptism in the Holy Spirit. I knew the baptism in the Holy Spirit was another step into my journey of getting to know Jesus intimately. I would enter into another dimension of the treasure of His Presence in my life.

Acts 19: 6

And when Paul had laid hands on them, the Holy Spirit came upon them, and they spoke with tongues and prophesied.

One night, I had friends from the church I was attending visit me in my home. They began to pray with me to receive the baptism in the Holy Spirit. As we prayed, I began by faith to speak in tongues. There were no fireworks or unusual displays of His Presence. It was by faith that I received and began to speak in tongues. This was the beginning of my spirit filled prayer life, a milestone in my journey of intimacy with Jesus. Since then, He would pour out His Spirit in my life in different measures.

There were times in my life when I did not feel as close to Him as other times. Most of those times, it was because I chose to walk my own way. Because He is faithful when we are not faithful, He would gently draw me close to Himself again and I would realign myself with Him (repent). Other times, it was simply a time of testing and in those times when I did not feel His Presence, I relied on His faithfulness not to leave me or forsake me; He **never** left me.

CHAPTER 5

The Candlestick

In the book of Exodus God gave instructions on how He wanted the Tabernacle built. The Tabernacle was built because God wanted a place to be able to meet with His people. Since the fall of man, God yearned and longed to dwell with man again. The Tabernacle was a temporary dwelling place for God's Presence on earth with His people until Jesus would make the way for His permanent dwelling in the heart of man.

Romans 15:4, states that everything written in the past was written to teach us something about our relationship with God in the present and the future. Therefore, the Tabernacle God instructed Moses to build can teach us many things about our relationship with God.

As I see it, the Tabernacle has three different spiritual depictions. It depicts our personal journey in our relationship with Jesus, the Court of Heaven, and also the stages of church history. I will be talking about the Tabernacle in regards to church history and our relationship with the Lord.

The physical Tabernacle had three sections, the Outer Court, the Holy Place and the Holy of Holies. The Outer Court is where the blood sacrifices were executed. It was where the Altar of Burnt Offerings was placed on which the sacrifices were performed for the atonement of sin. The Bronze Laver was also in the Outer Court for washing and cleansing which represents the cleansing and washing of sin through faith in the blood sacrifice of the Lamb.

Let me take a moment to testify of the power in the blood of Jesus our Passover Lamb. In Revelation 12:11 it states that we overcome him (Satan) by the blood of the Lamb and by the word of our testimony.

One night while I was sleeping, I was awakened from sleep and impressed by the Spirit to pray the blood of Jesus over my family and our home. My family was sleeping at the time and I said a short prayer to ask the Lord to cover us all and our home with His blood. Afterwards, I went right back to sleep. Awhile later the same night, I was awakened and startled by a piercing loud train like noise. It sounded like a train was going to plow right through our home. After a few minutes it was silent again and I went back to sleep. The next morning I woke up to find that my neighbors on each side of me had a tornado touchdown on their properties. The tornado touched my neighbor's house on the left side, jumped over my house, and touched my neighbor's house on the right side. It completely jumped over my house and nothing of my property was touched.

If I had not prayed the blood of Jesus over my family and home, I am certain the outcome would not have been the same. There is power in the blood of Jesus!

Another time when God demonstrated the power of the blood of Jesus in my life was a few years later. I had a fear of staying by myself at night. My husband at the time worked offshore in the Gulf of Mexico. Every time he would leave to go to work, I would gather my children and go to grandma's to sleep for the night. Well, needless to say, this started to get old. I prayed and asked the Lord to take this fear from me. After I prayed about it, I came across a small book on the power of the blood of Jesus. I began to read it and in prayer, I would apply the blood of Jesus to myself when I was alone at night. After a couple of nights of applying the blood of Jesus, I was set free from that fear. I began to stay home with my children in peace from that time on experiencing healing and deliverance as well as salvation through the power of His blood. The blood of the sacrificial Lamb is what gives us access not only to cleansing and salvation but also to the power of God.

In the same way God delivered the children of Israel because the blood was applied to the door post of their homes, He delivered me. (Exodus 12: 13 & 14)

In the Tabernacle, there was only one door to enter into the Holy Place from the Outer Court which depicts Jesus being the one and only Door and the only Way to the Father.

John 10:9-10

"I am the door, if anyone enters by Me, he will be saved, and will go in and out and find pasture. The thief does not come except to steal, and to kill, and to destroy. I have come that they may have life, and that they may have it more abundantly."

The Holy Place was the middle section. It was the section where the priest ministered to the Lord after the blood sacrifice was made. Only the priest could enter the Holy Place which is representative of those of us who have been washed in the blood of Jesus. In Revelation 5:9 & 10 it states that those of us who are washed in the blood of Jesus are Kings and Priests unto our God. We enter into a relationship with our Father through the one and only Door which is Jesus, our sacrificial Lamb, as Kings and Priests unto God.

The gold Candlestick (Menorah), the Table of Showbread and the Altar of Incense were the three pieces of furniture in the Holy Place. These three pieces of furniture depict specific purposes. The Candlestick represents the fire and light of the Holy Spirit, the baptism in the Holy Spirit, the seven spirits of God and illumination or revelation. It depicts Jesus in the midst of His church enlightening His Church with the light of His Presence.

The Menorah has 7 candlesticks made from one solid piece. The middle candlestick depicts Jesus and the six others have their flame in the direction of the middle candlestick which illustrates the Holy Spirit and the church always glorifying and looking to Jesus.

Revelation 21:23 says that the New Jerusalem has no need for the sun or the moon because the Lamb is its lamp. Jesus is our light!

John 1:1

In the beginning was the Word, and the Word was with God, and the Word was God.

John 6:35

And Jesus said to them, "I am the bread of life. He who comes to Me shall never hunger, and he who believes in Me shall never thirst."

The Table of Showbread was a small table with 12 loaves of bread. It represents Jesus being the Bread of life who was broken for us. Also, it represents the body of Christ in unity of fellowship sharing the Word of God, Jesus being the Word. The church is to be nurtured and feed by the Word of God in order to grow and thrive.

The Altar of Incense was a golden altar that sat in front of the curtain or veil which separated the Holy Place from the Holy of Holies. The Altar represents prayer, intercession and worship continually rising to the Father as a sweet aroma. The fire and incense on the altar was not to go out day or night. (Rev. 8:3-5)

The Holy of Holies was beyond the veil where the manifest glory of His Presence rested. The veil was for the purpose of separating sinful man from a Holy God. It was for man's protection because sin could not exist behind the veil. But, in Jesus Christ, God dealt with the sin that separated Him from His people.

When I was about 17 years of age while lying on my sofa in my living room, I fell asleep. I began to dream that I was on the sofa trying to stand up and Satan was sitting on the edge. In my dream, I kept trying to get up off the sofa but every time I would try Satan would push me back down. This happened repeatedly all the while Satan was laughing at me. I woke up from my dream and while I was awake, suddenly, appeared a picture of a Menorah before me. Now you have to understand, I wasn't saved but about a year and I knew very little about the Bible and spiritual things. I had never experienced a vision before. I didn't even understand at the time that I was having a vision. When I saw the Menorah, I had no idea what it was. I was perplexed and mystified as to what this could be and why I was seeing it.

As time passed, I forgot about the vision. A year or so later I was looking at a book and saw a picture of a Menorah in the book. When I saw the picture, I remembered seeing it in the vision but still didn't realize at the time it was a vision. In the book, I read that it was called a Menorah which is a Jewish candlestick. Later, I discovered what the Menorah represented in the Tabernacle God instructed Moses to build. I began to understand that it was actually a vision God had given me. I was still puzzled as to why He gave me this vision. What was His purpose in showing me the Menorah? God always does what He does for a specific purpose. He is never hap-hazard.

As time passed, He began to show me the purpose of the vision. As I said previously, I began to understand that the Tabernacle is a depiction of the church era in God's timeline and also a depiction of our personal relationship with Him. It is the blue print to enter into and live in His Presence.

As for Church history, the outer court depicts the time of Jesus when He gave His life and shed His blood as our final and ultimate sacrifice for sin. The Holy Place depicts the last days. The last days began with the resurrection of Christ and ends with the second coming of Christ. We are in the era of the last days. If the last days started at the resurrection, then you can understand, two thousand years later, we are much closer to the return of Christ. Time is short!

The Holy of Holies, in Church History, represents the time when the church is raptured and Jesus snatches His Bride up into the Heavenly Jerusalem where we will dwell in His Presence for eternity. Come Lord Jesus!

Hebrews 6:19

This hope we have as an anchor of the soul, both sure and steadfast, and which enters the Presence behind the veil.

In the Old Testament, only the High Priest was allowed to go behind the veil, and only once a year. They would go beyond the veil into the manifest glory of His Presence. It was not taken lightly.

When Jesus was crucified, the veil was torn in two from top to bottom. This signified that the way into the Father's Presence or into the Holy of Holies had been made for all men to enter in. It isn't just a select few any longer; we all have the hope of being able to enter into His Presence today.

The Menorah was placed in the Holy Place, which is the middle portion of the Tabernacle, for specific reasons. One reason being, we are in the last days when God wants to pour out His Spirit in fullness. He is going to illuminate His church with wisdom in the revelation of the knowledge of God like never before. Signs, wonders and miracles will be commonplace. We will be awe struck at what God is going to do because of the unusual power He will display.

In the Body of Christ some stop at salvation, the outer court experience. However, God has so much more for us. His desire is that we know Him in a much deeper and maximum way. His sacrifice paid the price for us to be able to know and experience Him in His fullness. After salvation, through the Blood of Jesus, we have access to the baptism or infilling of the Holy Spirit. Don't stop at the outer court; go further and deeper. Seek Him and you will find Him.

I was once asked, "If you had one thing to ask God for, what would it be?" My answer was, "ALL." I want all of what His death purchased for me, all of who He is, all of His fullness and all of His benefits.

His death paid the price for us to enjoy and experience ALL of who He is. Not to enjoy all, would be to undermine the price He paid. If you were to pay the maximum price for the most extravagant gift you could give to someone you love and they didn't enjoy or utilize that gift to the fullest, that would disappoint you, wouldn't it? It doesn't compare to the price our Father paid to give us the gift of life in His Presence. It grieves our Father to pay such a price for the gift He has made available to us and we not enjoy and utilize that gift to the fullest. It is our Father's good pleasure to give us His Kingdom.

The Holy Place is the place in our relationship with the Lord, where the Blood of Christ, the Holy Spirit, the Word and prayer bring us through the sanctification process in order to stand before our God unashamed and with confidence. Sanctification is the process in which God makes one holy and sets one apart for His use. He will test us in the fire of trials to purify us. If we are in Christ, we are being sanctified. That process isn't always easy. As a matter of fact, it is usually trying.

In order for God to do what He wants to do in us and through us, He will bring us to a place of unity and richness in the Spirit and in the Word, which the Menorah and Table of Showbread represents. That will bring us to a place of prophetic, anointed and unceasing intercession, praise, and worship which the Altar of Incense depicts.

As a result, we will be brought into the glory of His Presence unveiled, which is represented by the Holy of Holies, with His glory being revealed in us and through us in the earth.

Isaiah 11:2

The Spirit of the Lord shall rest upon Him, the Spirit of wisdom and understanding, the Spirit of counsel and might, the Spirit of knowledge and of the fear of the Lord.

The Church will grow in the fullness of the Spirit functioning in the 7 characteristics of the seven Spirits of God. These expressions are: **1)** The Spirit of the Lord, **2)** The Spirit of Wisdom, **3)** The Spirit of Understanding, **4)** The Spirit of Counsel, **5)** The Spirit of Power, **6)** The Spirit of Knowledge of God, **7)** and the Spirit of the Fear of the Lord. The Church will walk in such a way that will display these features to the world in an undeniable fashion.

One purpose in Jesus coming as a man was to show us how to walk as men and women in the fullness of the Spirit of God. Just as He walked as a man in the fullness of the Spirit, we too as mere men and women can walk in Him and through Him. As the Body of Christ does this, the Glory of His Presence will be poured out through the church to reveal Christ to the world.

In the Tabernacle, you see our journey in His Presence going from glory to glory, one dimension of His Presence into another. Starting at the Outer Court (washed by the blood of the Lamb) into the Holy Place (filled with the Holy Spirit and the Word to fulfill our role in prayer, worship and intercession) and ultimately into His Glory unveiled (the Holy of Holies). Not until Jesus's death and resurrection, were we able to enter into His Presence unveiled. Remember, in Moses' day, only the High Priest could enter beyond the veil and only once a year.

The only thing that has changed in the inner court with the death and resurrection of Christ is the veil. It was ripped from top to bottom, which affirms we not only have access to heaven if we die in Christ but we will in these last days be able to enter into the Glory of His Presence and release it to the world around us. His unveiled Presence is for us to experience here and now, not only *to* us but *through* us.

The Candlestick, the Table of Showbread, and the Altar of Incense remained unchanged. The washing of the blood of Jesus, the Holy Spirit, the fellowship of the church in the Word, prayer, intercession and worship are all still vital to our spiritual life. They are essential to living in His Presence.

The Menorah was the only source of light in the Holy Place which the Priest would need in order to commune with God at the Table of Showbread and the Altar of Incense. This signifies the importance of the Holy Spirit in our relationship with God.

In John 16:7-14 Jesus talks about the importance of the Holy Spirit's role in revealing Jesus and the Father to the world and to His people. The Holy Spirit draws us to Jesus, the Holy Spirit reveals Jesus and the Holy Spirit magnifies and glorifies Jesus.

The Spirit of God is necessary to enter into an intimate and experiential knowledge of Jesus. He illuminates the Word of God (Table of Showbread) giving revelation in the knowledge of God and unveiling the glory of God which is the intention of the veil being ripped in half.

The Holy Spirit brings forth true worship and prayer which is represented in the Altar of Incense. In John 4:24, Jesus said, "they that worship Him must worship Him in spirit and truth." Also, in Romans 8:26 Paul says, "for we know not what we should pray for as we ought but the spirit itself makes intercession for us with groanings we cannot utter."

So you see, we need God the Holy Spirit in order to know God. In 1 Corinthians 2:10, it says only the Spirit of God can reveal the heart of God. It takes God to know God. We can do nothing without Him.

Accepting the blood sacrifice of Jesus, the Lamb of God, for the remission of our sin is only the beginning. His blood sacrifice (The Outer Court) gives us access and entrance (The Door) into the privilege of getting to know Him in an experiential way (The Holy Place).

We can see the Trinity in the Tabernacle; Jesus, in the sacrificial lamb, the Holy Spirit in the Menorah, and the Father in the Holy of Holies. We can't have one without the other.

I was born again at the time of my dream and the vision, but I needed the baptism of the Holy Spirit to give me the power to overcome in this life and to know Him intimately. This is what the Lord was saying to me in the vision.

In Zechariah 4:6 the Lord's message to Zerubbabel was, "Not by might, nor by power, but by My Spirit, says the Lord of Hosts." We can't do anything without the Spirit of God. He is our helper, He is our strength. Grace is dispensed through the Holy Spirit, without Him there is no grace to overcome in this world.

Jeremiah 2:13 says, "They have forsaken Me, the Spring of Living Water." There are many of us and churches that have excluded the Holy

Spirit and as a result, we live defeated lives with no power. We cannot make it in our own strength. This is what the Lord is saying to the church. This is what He was saying when He instructed Moses to put the candlestick in the Holy Place.

1 Corinthians 3:16

Know ye not that ye are the temple of God, and that the Spirit of God dwelleth in you?

This may blow your mind: We, the people of God, are the temple of God made without hands, formed by the Spirit of God. It is Christ in you and me the hope of glory. We have the Light of His Spirit within. The Church is to be filled richly with the Spirit, the Word and prayer. He wants to overflow from within us to be released to the world around us. The candlestick depicts the people of God filled with the light of His Presence in a dark world.

In Zechariah 4:1-7, Zechariah saw a vision of the Menorah. God gave the vision and the message to Zechariah for Zerubbabel. The Angel of the Lord told Zechariah what the interpretation of the vision was.

The mountains in our lives will be brought low by the Spirit of the Lord in us. Mountains refer to the struggles, difficulties and the impossibilities we face in life. Not by our own strength, wisdom or efforts, but by the strength and power of the Spirit of the Lord in us and through us. Without Him, we *cannot* and He *will not* without us. It is through His Spirit that grace is dispensed or administered to enable us to live a victorious life over sin, trials and enemies.

Matthew 5:14-16 Jesus says, *"You are the light of the world. A city that is set on a hill cannot be hidden. Nor do they light a lamp and put it under a basket, but on a lampstand, and it gives light to all who are in the house. Let your light so shine before men, that they may see your good works and glorify your Father in heaven."*

It is imperative that the people of God partner with Him, working with Him as opposed to for Him. In the book of Acts starting with chapter 1, we see Jesus telling His disciples to wait for the promise of the Father. That promise was the Holy Spirit. Jesus told them that they would receive power when the Holy Spirit would come upon them.

Acts 2:1-4

When the Day of Pentecost had fully come, they were all with one accord in one place. Suddenly there came a sound from heaven, as of a rushing mighty wind, and it filled the whole house where they were sitting. Then there appeared to them divided tongues, as of fire, and one sat upon each of them. They were all filled with the Holy Spirit and began to speak with other tongues, as the Spirit gave them utterance.

When the disciples received the Holy Spirit and the Fire of the Spirit rested on each of their heads they became living lampstands or candlesticks. It wasn't until then that they were given the power to be light to the world. It wasn't until then that they were given power to work signs, miracles and wonders. Then and only then were they able to change the world around them and endure the hardship they went through.

Acts 2:16-21

But this is what was spoken by the prophet Joel: it shall come to pass in the last days, says God, that I will pour out of My Spirit on all flesh; Your sons and your daughters shall prophesy, your young men shall see visions, Your old men shall dream dreams. On My menservants and on My maidservants I will pour out My Spirit in those days; they shall prophesy. I will show wonders in heaven above and signs in the earth beneath: Blood and fire and vapor of smoke. The sun shall be turned into darkness, the moon into blood, before the coming of the great and awesome day of the Lord. It shall come to pass that whoever calls on the name of the Lord shall be saved.

This is what God wants to do in us and through us. He wants you and me to be living lampstands or candlesticks burning with the fire and power of the Holy Spirit. It is how we will thrive and make an impact in our homes, our grocery stores and our work places. This Promise is an inheritance for us and our children.

What can we learn from the Tabernacle for our lives today? 1) We are required to repent of sin in our lives. 2) Know that the blood of Jesus our sacrificial Lamb is what will wash and cleanse us of sin (the Outer Court). 3) Be filled with the Spirit of God continually (the Menorah). 4) Feed on the Word of God daily (Table of Showbread). 5) Worship Him in prayer and intercession (Altar of Incense). 6) Then, we will be ushered into the Glory of His Presence unveiled (the Holy of Holies) with His power and might to touch and influence the world around us.

John 1:14

And the Word became flesh and dwelt among us, and we beheld His glory, the glory as of the only begotten of the Father, full of grace and truth.

Zechariah 4: 7

Who are you, O Great Mountain? Before Zerubbabel you shall become a plain! And he shall bring forth the capstone with shouts of "Grace, grace to it!"

Being filled with His Spirit, gives us the grace and the power to be like Him, to walk like Him and to love like Him. As it says in the book of Zechariah, we can then shout: Grace! Grace! To the mountains in our lives in the power of the Holy Spirit and they will be no more.

The priests, when they went into the Holy Place to minister to the Lord, had to make sure there was oil at all times in the candlestick and they had to trim the lamps to make sure the fire would burn continually. We too, as priests of the Most High, must tend to our hearts to ensure we have the oil of the Spirit in constant supply so the fire of His Spirit will burn unceasingly.

We must trim our lamps making sure we trim away the dead works of sin from our lives and keep our hearts pure before the Lord in repentance thereby we keep the fire of the Holy Spirit burning in our lives.

Just as God gave Zechariah this message through a vision of the Menorah, He is giving it today.

CHAPTER 6

Ten Virgins

Matthew 25:1-13 speaks about the 10 virgins, of whom five were wise and five were foolish. The wise virgins had stored up oil and the foolish virgins did not.

The foolish virgins squandered the opportunities they had to store up the oil, so much so they were found with none and when they needed it the most they were empty. When their Bridegroom came, they were not permitted to enter through the door because they had no oil.

I believe this is a picture of some of us in the church today. We have been foolish and squandered the most precious treasure man could ever possess, the *Treasure* of A*ll Treasures*. We have squandered the Holy Spirit right out of the midst of our churches; therefore we are weak, defeated, and powerless to affect the world around us.

Jesus is coming soon. The world is in perilous times. The Lord is calling us to awaken, prepare, trim our lamps and be filled with oil as wise virgins. As the days get darker in these end times, we will need the power and grace of God more than ever. That grace and power comes by and through the Holy Spirit. We should never disregard the Holy Spirit, and **now**, is not the time to exclude the third person of the Godhead.

In Revelation 2:4-5, the Lord is speaking to the church. He says, *"Nevertheless I have this against you, that you have left your first love. Remember therefore from where you have fallen; repent and do the first works, or else I will come to you quickly and remove your lampstand from its place—unless you repent."*

Unless we are diligent to keep our first Love in God, to trim our lamps, and keep them full of the oil of His Spirit, our lamps will be taken. His Presence will be lifted. What then will we have? We will have dry, cold, hopeless, and powerless religion that benefits no one.

2 Corinthians 3:5 & 6

Not that we are sufficient of ourseleves to think of anything as being from ourselves, but our sufficiency is from God, who also made us sufficient as ministers of the new covenant, not of the letter but of the Spirit; for the letter kills, but the Spirit gives life.

Our sufficiency is not of ourselves; it is from God. We begin and maintain a relationship with Him through His Grace which is given by the working of the Holy Spirit in our lives. In John 15:5, Jesus said that He is the Vine and we are the branches; apart from Him we can do nothing.

In 2 Corinthians 3:6 it says, *"The letter kills, but the Spirit gives life."* This is an issue of life or death. The Spirit supplies the power we need to live and overcome in this world.

I pray that we all understand the seriousness of the hour we live in. As wise virgins, let us store up the oil of His Presence in our hearts and lives so we can become burning and living lamps in this dark world.

When the time comes to give oil to those who are searching and crying out for deliverance, we must be ready. We must be ready to stand and take back the ground that we so carelessly squandered away. At the return of the Lord, we do not want the door shut on us, as the foolish virgins.

Job 22:21

Now acquaint yourself with Him, and be at peace; thereby good will come to you.

Let us acquaint ourselves or agree and align ourselves with the Lord. In order to agree, you have to know what He is saying. Once you know what He is saying, you can agree; once you agree, you can align yourself and then, you will be blessed with great good.

Stepping out to obey the Lord can be very scary at times. It's common to fear the unknown. Often the Lord will ask us to step out into the unknown, and if you take that first step to obey, He will meet you. Sometimes we have to step out in the face of fear and once we do, God will be there. Choosing to do what is right in the midst of fear is called courage.

I remember the first time I taught an adult Bible class of about 100 people. I was terrified! When I took the first step to obey, He met me. As I continued, I began to be more and more comfortable with teaching.

God blessed my obedience and others were blessed as a result. Stepping out to write and publish this book was scary! Don't let fear stop you from your purpose and destiny in God. Our obedience affects the world around us, as well as, our own life. Let us be as wise virgins keeping our lamps trimmed and filled with oil to be found ready.

CHAPTER 7

Revival Outpouring

Several years past, I heard of a church in Pensacola Florida where God was pouring out His Spirit in unusual ways. I heard of miracles happening and Jesus revealing Himself in many tangible ways. I was drawn to go there because I was hungry to know God. The church I was attending at the time had several people going to this church in Florida, so I jumped on board. The things I saw and experienced were awe inspiring.

Little did I know, I would experience God in a way that not many people have. Since then, I have never been the same. I entered into another dimension of prayer and intercession I had never experienced before.

I felt closer to Jesus than ever before. His Presence was so tangible at times I would feel like I was on fire. When I say fire, it was by no means a tormenting or hurtful sensation. The best way I can describe it is that it was an exhilarating intense passion for Jesus and the things of God. When the Lord would pour out His Spirit, miracles would happen, people would get set free from bondage, they were healed and born again.

One particular time after revival service, I went to shake the hand of a lady just to say hello. As we shook hands, she fell to the ground and shouted, "She has electricity coming through her hands!" The Presence and power of God was so strong that it knocked her to the ground. I didn't feel it, but she did. She was blessed beyond measure at the power of God she experienced.

Before I went to revival, I had never taught officially in a church setting. I was insecure and never spoke in public. After I received that outpouring of the Holy Spirit, the Lord empowered me by His Spirit to teach and preach. He used me to bring forth His Word that would set people free and draw them closer to Jesus.

I grew exponentially in and because of His Presence in my life. With Him, we can do things we would not otherwise be able to do. He changes us for the better. We *can't* do it without Him; He *won't* do it without us.

CHAPTER 8

The Sunflower

Isaiah 61:1-3

The Spirit of the Lord God is upon Me, because the Lord has anointed Me, to preach good tidings to the poor; He has sent Me, to heal the brokenhearted, to proclaim liberty to the captives and the opening of the prison to those who are bound; to proclaim the acceptable year of the Lord, and the day of vengeance of our God; to comfort all who mourn, to console those who mourn in Zion, to give them beauty for ashes, the oil of joy for mourning, the garment of praise for the spirit of heaviness; that they may be called trees of righteousness, the planting of the Lord, that He may be glorified."

Jesus is God's Anointed One who came to fulfill this prophecy in His life, death and resurrection. In Luke chapter four, Jesus affirmed that this was the essence of His ministry. It also describes the basic ministry He awarded to His church. His Presence transforms us into this very image if we are in the Son, align our will with His, and remain in Him.

Romans 8:29

For those whom He foreknew, He also destined from the beginning to be molded into the image of His Son that He might become the firstborn of many brethren.

One morning I was at my kitchen counter eating sunflower seeds and looking at the sunflowers I placed in different areas around my house. As I looked at them, the Lord spoke to me and said, "Let's talk about the sunflower." At that moment He began to lay out before me the parallel of the sunflower and being transformed into His image by His Presence.

The Lord said, "The sunflower personifies your relationship with Me and what My Presence will do in and through your life."

The word "flower" means, 'beauty, exact representation, to be in or reach an optimum stage of development' or 'to be developed fully and richly.' The name sunflower refers to the beauty of or exact representation of the sun. The beauty and the reflection of the sun emanate from the sunflower. The sunflower must remain in the sun to be transformed into the reflection of the sun.

Jesus said in John 15:4- 5, *"Abide in Me, and I in you. As the branch cannot bear fruit of itself, unless it abides in the vine, neither can you, unless you abide in Me. I am the vine, you are the branches. He who abides in Me, and I in him, bears much fruit; for without Me you can do nothing."*

He also said in Matthew 13:43 that the righteous will shine forth as the sun in the kingdom of their Father.

In John 14:9 Jesus is telling His disciples that He is the exact image of the Father. If you see Jesus, you see the Father. He is the reflection of the Father, reflecting the beauty of the Father because He abides in the Father. In the same way as Jesus is in the Father and the sunflower is in the sun, we too must abide in the Son to reflect His image and His beauty on earth.

1John 4:17

Love has been perfected among us in this: that we may have boldness in the Day of Judgment: because as He is, so are we in this world.

The goal is to be the reflection of Christ in every way, reflecting His love, humility, joy, peace, and authority to set the captive free. You may be thinking it is an impossible task and it is within our own strength. But, with God all things are possible. It is Christ who works in us the will and the ability to do His good pleasure. He turns our ashes into beauty!!

Born Again

John 3:3

Jesus answered and said to him, "Most assuredly, I say to you, unless one is born again, he cannot see the kingdom of God."

Without new birth, there is no life and no relationship with God. Just as the sunflower seed must be buried in the earth and die to itself, we must die to the old man and live in Christ as a new creation. We must be born again.

We must be born of our mother's womb which is the first birth. The second birth is being born again into the Son which is the first impartation or introduction into His Presence. The Spirit of God then takes His place within our earthen vessel.

Baptism In The Holy Spirit

Joel 2: 23

Be glad then, you children of Zion, and rejoice in the Lord your God for He has given you the former rain faithfully, and He will cause the rain to come down for you…

The sunflower must have rain to grow and bring forth the image of the sun. After we are born again, we must have the rain of His Presence to water and refresh us as we grow in this parched world. If not, we dry up and die just as the sunflower would without rain.

In Joel, rain refers to His Presence being poured out or raining upon us and refreshing us. The sunflower needs rain on a regular basis in order to grow and produce. In the same way, we need the rain of His Presence on a regular basis to grow and produce the image of Christ. Just as the earth does not hold its water, neither do we. As earthen vessels, we leak, and we need to be refreshed regularly with the rain of His Presence to stay healthy and vibrant. This keeps us dependent on Him daily. He created us to need Him continually. He is the potter, and we are the clay.

2 Corinthians 4:7

But we have this treasure in earthen vessels, that the excellence of the power may be of God and not of us.

Life can be draining; it can wear us down, leave us feeling empty, alone, and hopeless. The daily refreshing of His Presence strengthens us and empowers us to continue facing the challenges each day brings.

Jesus mentioned that we would have trials and tribulations in this world but to be of good cheer because He has overcome the world. His Presence gives us the joy we need in this life to face challenges and difficulties.

The Fruit Of The Spirit

The sunflower produces its seeds as it is transformed by the sun and the rain. I happen to love sunflower seeds. Not only do they taste great, they also have lots of nourishment. Just as the sunflower produces fruit, we should be producing the fruit of the Holy Spirit in our lives. As others experience the Presence of God and the fruit of His Spirit in our life, it will bring nourishment and life to their souls. Then, we can truly say, *taste and see that the Lord is good.*

Galatians 5:22- 23

But the fruit of the Spirit is love, joy, peace, longsuffering, kindness, goodness, faithfulness, gentleness, self-control. Against such there is no law.

I Corinthians 3:6-9 talks about how we are to plant and water spiritual seed. As we spread joy, hope and love to others, we are planting seeds of His Presence. Good and loving deeds release the Presence of God on the earth eventually reaping a harvest of souls.

In the book of Matthew, after His resurrection, Jesus tells His disciples to go and make disciples of all nations. His Presence not only transforms us, but He will transform the lives of those around us. In writing this book, I am planting seeds for all who are willing to enjoy the fruit of His Presence and God will give the increase.

...not make seeds grow. All we
...and water; if we do, God will
...ase. Let it go and let God.

...wer doesn't have to work and toil to
...er; it just is. A flower is a flower
...e of the elements it lives in. The sun, rain
...oil produce a flower. As we live in the Son,
...rain of the Holy Spirit, and the soil of the
...ord of God, we will just be, without trying in
our own strength.

The sunflower is bright and bold; it brings life, joy and nourishment to those who eat its fruit.

We too, must display the brightness of His light, be bold, and bring joy and nourishment to the world around us. Then, we can truly say, we are His *sonflower!!*

CHAPTER 9

Strength in Our Weakness

Psalm 89:17 says that the Lord is the glory of our strength. Through my life and in my walk with the Lord, I have had many difficult challenges, as most of us. People would comment on how strong they thought I was. I would think to myself just the opposite because I was very aware of my frailty and my weakness. I would question as to how they could say they saw me as strong. At a moment when I questioned this in my heart, the Lord spoke to me. He said, "They see My strength working in you. Because you realize your weakness and you rely on Me, My strength is made perfect in your weakness. My strength covers your weakness as long as you rely on Me to be your strength." He is faithful! He is not limited by our limitations when we rely on Him. Understanding our frailty, weakness, and absolute dependency on Him, is when we tap into His strength.

2 Corinthians 12:9- 10

And He said to me, "My grace is sufficient for you, for My strength is made perfect in weakness," Therefore most gladly I will rather boast in my infirmities, that the power of Christ may rest (pitch a tent) upon me. Therefore, I take pleasure in infirmities, in reproaches, in needs, in persecutions, in distresses, for Christ's sake. For when I am weak, then I am strong.

The word "rest" actually means, 'to pitch a tent.' In our weakness, troubles, and tribulations, Jesus pitches a tent in them with us. If we allow Him, He will be our strength. He is not looking in from the outside of our trials. He is in them with us to stay until He gets us through them. Along the way His strength is being made perfect in us. As we give the Holy Spirit His rightful place in our lives, even in the midst of hardship, the grace we need, at the time we need it, is dispensed to strengthen us and the mountains are made low. His Presence sustains us through the hardships while we are becoming His *sonflower*.

CHAPTER 10

Through the Fire

Daniel 3:1-28

Allow the trials, challenges and heartbreak of this life to propel you into His Presence for safety and victory. Allow them to thrust you into a more intimate relationship with His Presence, which is where you will gain victory. In His Presence is where the trials are used to mold us into His image, and we come out of the fire without one hair of our heads singed or the smell of smoke on our lives.

I was talking with a lady in a church I had gone to years ago; she didn't know any of my history. She mentioned to me that it didn't look like I had really gone through any difficult times in my life. To be honest, I was offended by her comment. I said to the Lord, "Now Lord, that lady doesn't know me or anything about my life. She upset me." Well, just as the Lord so sweetly does, He used this opportunity to teach me something.

He said, "The reason she can't see any evidence of you ever going through the fire is because I was in it with you and I brought you out just like I did Shadrach, Meshach, and Abednego in Daniel Chapter 3." They were thrown into a fiery furnace that was turned up seven times hotter than usual because of their faith in God. Suddenly, the Son of God was found to be in the fire with them. He pitched His tent in the fire with them.

The four of them were walking in the midst of the fire with no harm to them. When they came out of the furnace, those around them witnessed that the fire had no power to harm them. The hair on their head was not singed nor their garments affected by the smell of the fire.

He will be with us in the fire and will bring us through the fire without any evidence of the fire on our lives. The one thing it will do if we allow it is bring us into a more intimate relationship with Jesus. More importantly than just getting us through the hardships of life, His Presence forms and molds us into His image with the beauty of Christ shining through us as a testimony to the world. People will be drawn to that beauty just as I was drawn to the beauty of the sunflower.

Becoming acquainted with His Presence is what will bring forth the beauty of the image of the

Son in our lives. It is what will bring the Kingdom of God in our lives and to the lives of those around us. Then, we can say we are His *sonflower!!*

CHAPTER 11

Peace Only He Gives

Philippians 4:7

And the peace of God, which surpasses all understanding, will guard your hearts and minds through Christ Jesus.

Ephesians 2:14

For He Himself is our peace, who has made both one, and has broken down the middle wall of separation.

John 14:27

Peace I leave with you, My peace I give to you; not as the world gives do I give to you. Let not your heart be troubled, neither let it be afraid.

We are all constantly looking and striving to gain peace in our hearts and minds. Many of us look in so many different places to find peace that will quiet our hearts and minds but find disappointment instead. Until we experience Him and come to know Jesus, we will fall short of the peace we so desperately need.

Jesus is our peace! He made peace available to us by His sacrifice. He has ripped in two the veil that separates us from Him and abolished in His flesh the veil of division.

He purchased peace for us on the cross. Peace is a promise to those of us who are in right relationship with Him. Before I came to the

Lord, I was frantically looking for relief. It wasn't until I encountered Jesus and gave my life to Him that I found true peace. As I became more familiar with Him and His Presence in my life, that peace grew. He took the guilt, shame, fear and condemnation and replaced it with His peace.

When I was in my early twenties, I had problems sleeping at night. I had asked my Pastor to pray for me. After she prayed with me, that night, I felt peace I had never felt before and I slept better than ever before. Jesus gave me peace beyond what I could understand.

Isaiah 53:5

But He was wounded for our transgressions, He was bruised for our iniquities; The chastisement for our peace was upon Him, and by His stripes we are healed.

The suffering, humiliation and rejection *we deserve,* He took upon Himself and in return He gives us what *we don't deserve.* It is called the great exchange-- He takes what we deserve and He gives what we don't deserve.

He promises to be the Prince of Peace in our lives, but we must make Him Prince in order to possess His peace. There is no peace in the areas He is not allowed to reign as Prince. I pray His Presence is allowed to consume all aspects of your being that He would reign as Prince of Peace in all things concerning you.

Shalom is Hebrew for the peace of God. In Jesus you have shalom which means wholeness, completeness, soundness, welfare, and prosperity. If you have Him, you have shalom because He is shalom.

CHAPTER 12

Focus

What we focus on is what we will attract. When we focus on Jesus and the things of God, that is what we will attract into our lives. We empower what we focus on. This is why Paul instructs us to be renewed in our minds.

Philippians 4:8

Finally, brethren, whatever things are true, whatever things are noble, whatever things are just, whatever things are pure, whatever things are lovely, whatever things are of good report, if there is any virtue and if there is anything praiseworthy—meditate on these things.

Romans 12:2

And do not be conformed to this world, but be transformed by the renewing of your mind, that you may prove what is that good and acceptable and perfect will of God.

Our minds are the property of the Lord Jesus Christ. We are to purposefully submit them to Him daily, focusing on Him and His kingdom.

1 Peter 1:13

Therefore gird up the loins of your mind, be sober, and rest your hope fully upon the grace that is to be brought to you at the revelation of Jesus Christ;

Peter instructs us to gird up our mind. To "gird up" implies, 'to surround' or 'encompass'. It also means, 'to secure.' We are to surround and encompass our minds with the Gospel, thereby securing our minds with the mind of Christ.

When a soldier would go to battle he would secure or gird up his sword to his body before battle knowing that he would be defeated without it.

In the same way, we are to gird up our minds with the Sword of the Spirit which is the Word of God. Without it, we would be defeated by the enemy and the world.

In every situation and circumstance the enemy is fighting for center stage. He is fighting for our minds, and if we focus on him, the world and circumstances around us, we give place to him. The enemy would like nothing better than to get our focus off of Jesus; He knows if he can do that the battle for him is won.

If we want to experience the kingdom of God, we focus on the kingdom of God. We have a choice, choose Jesus. Let Him have His rightful place in your focus and you will experience His peace and it will reign in your heart and mind.

CHAPTER 13

Drawing Near

There are several ways in which we draw near to the Lord. First, we must realize God Himself must first give us the desire to draw near to Him. Even to have the desire to draw near to God comes from God, because all good things come from Him. If you find that you have no desire, ask Him and He will give it because it is His desire. If we draw near to Him, He will draw near to us (James 4:8).

Drawing Near Through Repentance

Repentance is represented by the Altar of Sacrifice and the Bronze Laver in the Outer Court of the Tabernacle.

James 4:8

Draw near to God and He will draw near to you. Cleanse your hands, you sinners; and purify your hearts, you double minded.

Repentance of sin is not just being remorseful. Repentance is a godly sorrow which causes us to turn away from sin and align our life with God in humility. Remember, He abides with those of a humble and repentant heart. Simply put, humility is knowing your need of God.

John 6:44

"No one can come to Me unless the Father who sent Me draws him;

Romans 2:4

Or do you despise the riches of His goodness, forbearance, and longsuffering, not knowing that the goodness of God leads you to repentance?

He has done all that is necessary to reconcile us to Himself. He gives us the faith, He draws us by His spirit, and He continually pours out His goodness towards us to compel us to surrender to Him. He does everything for us except make the choice to surrender. Making the choice must be an act of our own free will. That, He *will not* do for us.

Hebrews 10: 19

Therefore brethren, having boldness to enter the Holiest, His Presence, by the blood of Jesus

Once our conscience and hearts are cleansed with His blood, we can come boldly without shame into His Presence to obtain the grace and mercy we need.

Drawing Near Through His Word

The Word is represented by the table of Showbread in the Holy Place.

2 Corinthians 3:18

And all of us, as with unveiled face, as we continue to behold the Word of God as in a mirror the glory of the Lord, are constantly being transfigured into His very own image in ever increasing splendor and from one degree of glory to another: for this comes from the Lord Who is the Spirit.

We draw near to Him as we are in His Word. We behold His beauty just as in a mirror and we are transformed into His image, one level of glory at a time, from glory to glory. As we see Jesus throughout scripture, our faith is increased; as our faith increases, we receive more of Him and give more of ourselves to Him. Faith, simply put, is enablement to receive from Him. When Jesus made this statement to His disciples, "ye of little faith", He was saying, "Why do you take so little of Me?" When the Spirit unveils Jesus throughout the Word, faith is ignited in our hearts to receive from Him what He has and wants to give. His Word is alive, powerful and able to change and create.

It isn't looking at ourselves that transforms us. The enemy tries to keep us looking at ourselves in self-centeredness and self-condemnation to keep us in bondage. It is beholding Jesus unveiled in the Word that transforms us into His image.

The Word of God is the only written source in which we can know what God thinks and says. It teaches us what God expects of us as well as what God has done and will do. It is God breathed and God inspired.

The Word of God is one of God's ways of releasing Himself into the earth. Read the Word, know the Word and speak the Word to release God into your life and the world around you.

Drawing Near Through Prayer

Prayer is represented by the Altar of Incense in the Holy Place.

It isn't necessarily the discipline of prayer that brings us into an intimate relationship with Him.

Many have a religious discipline of prayer and never come to know Him or experience His Presence. They engage in prayer as a spiritual slot machine hoping to get lucky and win the jack pot.

Coming before Him with a contrite heart of humility, wanting to know Him and experience Him is the heart and true purpose of prayer.

Drawing Near Through Praying In Tongues

The baptism in the Holy Spirit with the evidence of speaking in tongues is represented by the Menorah in the Holy Place.

Acts 2:4 says, "And they were all filled with the Holy Spirit and began to speak with other tongues, as the Spirit gave them utterance."

Romans 8:26 says, "Likewise the Spirit also helps in our weaknesses. For we do not know what we should pray for as we ought, but the

Spirit Himself makes intercession for us with groanings which cannot be uttered."

The disciples were afraid, weak, and hopeless after the death of Jesus. They were afraid to be seen in public much less speak in public. What was it that turned these weak cowardly disciples into courageous men and women with a fire and power in them to change the world? What was it that enabled them to look death in the face with no fear?

It was the baptism in the Holy Spirit with the evidence of speaking in tongues. It's the fire and power of the Spirit of God breathed in them and resting on them. They continued to be filled daily with the Spirit of God as they built themselves up in their prayer language. In 1 Corinthians 14:18 Paul says that he thanks God because he prays in tongues more than all of them.

When praying in tongues, you are giving place to the Spirit of God in your life that rightfully belongs to Him. As we pray in our prayer language the Spirit is praying perfectly through us. Praying in tongues stirs up the fire of the Spirit of God within us. It stirs up the gifts of God within us. Giving place to the Spirit of God makes available to us all the attributes of God as we need them.

Jude 1:20, 21

But you, beloved, building yourselves up on your most holy faith, praying in the Holy Spirit, keep yourselves in the love of God...

Praying in tongues is the love language of God. As you discipline yourself in praying in the Spirit, your intimacy with God grows deeper. You will find that your faith in God will grow, as well as the faith of God in you. When praying in tongues, you allow God the Holy Spirit to pray through you the knowledge and will of God. If you don't know how to pray the Holy Spirit does.

I want to encourage you to allow the Holy Spirit to have His place in your prayer time. You will find your relationship with the Lord more intimate and fulfilling. Praying in tongues allows the Holy Spirit to administer the grace we need to live according to the will of God.

Drawing Near Through Worship

Worship is also represented by the Altar of Incense in the Holy Place.

Worship and prayer are intertwined so much so you can barely tell them apart. Worship is much more than mere words of adoration. It is submitting one's life in obedience to the Father.

Genesis 22:5

And Abraham said to his young men, "Stay here with the donkey; the lad and I will go yonder and worship, and we will come back to you.

Isaac, Abraham's son, meant more to Abraham than Abraham's own life. In Genesis 22: 6 - 13, Abraham was willing to lay down everything, even his own son in obedience to God. In being willing to give Isaac to the Lord, Abraham was saying, "Lord, You mean more to me than my own life." This is true worship! God did not intend for Abraham to follow through and sacrifice his son. He was testing Abraham's dedication and loyalty. He stopped Abraham before Isaac was harmed because God Himself gave the sacrifice of His Son from the foundation of the world. (Revelation 13:8)

True worship is holding nothing back from Him and in turn He gives us all He is. If we lose our life for Him, we will gain it; if we save our life we lose it. (Matthew 10:39)

Drawing Near Through Fellowship

Fellowship with believers is represented by the Table of Showbread.

1Corinthians 12:20-21&27-28

But now indeed there are many members, yet one body. And the eye cannot say to the hand, "I have no need of you"; nor again the head to the feet, "I have no need of you."

Now you are the body of Christ, and members individually. God has appointed these in the church: first apostles, second prophets, third teachers, after that miracles, then gifts of healing, helps, administrations, varieties of tongues.

Hebrews 10:24 -25

And let us consider one another in order to stir up love and good works, not forsaking the assembling of ourselves together, as is the manner of some, but exhorting one another, and so much the more as you see the Day approaching.

Jesus made it very clear that He created us to need each other. We are the body of Christ. He has gifted each one of us with gifts that are for the edification of the Body in the faith. There is strength in numbers. We gather together to be strengthened by one another.

The gifts and talents He has placed in each one of us are to be used for the edification of others. They are not to be used to glorify ourselves but to glorify the Lord. There have been many occasions when I was going through a difficult time and the local church I was attending helped me through them. There were times when I needed to hear from God and He used someone in the local church to speak a word I needed to hear at that moment.

There was one particular time when I was experiencing excruciating back pain. I didn't know exactly what it was but the muscles in my back felt like noodles. It felt like they could not hold up my upper torso any longer. I decided to go to church even in the pain I was in. After the service was over, the Pastor had an altar call and I went up for prayer. Almost everyone had left and the Pastor was still at the altar praying. The Lord spoke to him and told him that there was someone with a muscle problem and God was healing them.

I didn't know exactly what was wrong with me but I knew I had a muscle problem and it was very painful. I knew God was speaking to me. I went home and the next day I was better and never had that particular pain again. Had I not gone to church, I wouldn't have received that word of healing. God uses His Body, the Church, to minister to one another. We sharpen one another as iron sharpens iron to smooth out our rough edges.

As we gather together, we complete one another as a Body. Our eye cannot say to our hand, I don't need you. Our head cannot say to our feet, I don't need you. (1 Corinthians 12: 20- 31) There is someone God placed in the local Body for you to help and minister to as well. On another occasion, I was in church at the altar praying for other people. My Pastor was praying with a man at the altar with his hand on the man's back. I walked behind the man and put my hand on top of my Pastor's hand to join him in prayer. As I did, the man felt what he called a jolt of lightning. He fell to the ground and had an encounter with the Holy Spirit. God revealed Himself to that man in a way that he would never forget.

I believe the Lord would have used someone else in that man's life if I were not there at that time, but I'm glad I was there to be used by God in his life.

The local Body is a place for your gift to be used to bless others. It is a place where you can grow in the ability to minister to others. It's an outlet for the Presence of God to flow through you as well as to you.

In early Church History the Body of Christ would meet in the synagogues regularly, but they gathered family and friends together weekly in individual homes to worship, teach, and minister to one another. As Christians, we are the Church, not the buildings we gather in. The home was the primary meeting place of the

Church and the main place of worship for early Christians.

This is why their children and children's children knew the Word and the Presence of God to pass on to the next generation. Our homes should still be our primary house of worship if we want to draw near to Him.

Drawing Near Through Giving

Malachi 3:10-12

Bring all the tithes into the storehouse, that there may be food in My house, and try Me now in this, Says the Lord of hosts, If I will not open for you the windows of heaven and pour out for you such blessing that there will not be room enough to receive it. And I will rebuke the devourer for your sakes, so that he will not destroy the fruit of your ground, nor shall the vine fail to bear fruit for you in the field, says the Lord. And all nations will call you blessed for you will be a delightful land says the Lord.

God actually invites us to prove Him in this—to prove His trustworthiness with our giving. He says those who give will be placed in a position under an open heaven where He will pour out His blessings. Not only provision for physical needs but His Spirit poured out as well.

God says that He will stop the devourer for our sakes when we give faithfully, so much so that Satan cannot stop the blessings of God from overtaking us.

It all belongs to the Lord. He doesn't so much need our money as He wants our obedience. The act of giving must come from a place of obedience and not from a place of giving to get. Our motive for giving should come from wanting to be a blessing in the Kingdom of God.

God always rewards obedience. The word "blessed" in Malachi 3:12 is defined as, 'being blessed in every sense of the word—spiritually, financially, emotionally and relational.'

Proverbs 3:9-10

Honor the Lord with your possessions and with the first fruits of all your increase; So your barns will be filled with plenty, and your vats will overflow with new wine.

This verse tells us as we give to God He will give us what we need physically to live and enough to give. New wine speaks of the Presence of the Holy Spirit. He will also give us an overflow of the Holy Spirit in our lives and enough to give.

Drawing Near Through Forgiveness

Matthew 6:14-15

For if you forgive men their trespasses, your heavenly Father will also forgive you. But if you do not forgive men their trespasses, neither will your Father forgive your trespasses.

Ephesians 4:31-32

Let all bitterness, wrath, anger, clamor, and evil speaking be put away from you, with all malice. And be kind to one another, tenderhearted, forgiving one another, even as God in Christ forgave you.

In God's word it is clear that God has no tolerance for unforgiveness. Just as He so graciously forgives us, He expects us to forgive others. If we have unforgiveness in our hearts towards anyone, we cannot expect to be forgiven and we will open ourselves up to oppression. I heard it put like this; unforgiveness is like drinking poison and expecting it to hurt someone else. In as much as we forgive others, God will forgive us. Through the blood of Jesus, we have God's permission to let go of all bitterness and resentment.

Forgiveness isn't a feeling; it's a choice to believe that we are forgiven by God and a choice to forgive others. Forgiveness is a major key to living in His Presence. Stop for a moment and consider your own hearts, if there is bitterness you are holding onto, forgive and let it go. It isn't worth the treasure of His Presence.

Drawing Near Through Blessing Israel

Genesis 12:3

I will bless those who bless you, and I will curse him who curses you; And in you all the families of the earth shall be blessed.

This is one reason for the rise and fall of nations. If a nation blesses Israel by standing with and befriending Israel, God blesses that nation with strength and prosperity. God Himself will be the friend of the nation that is the friend of Israel. (John 15:14)

It is important for us to understand the significance Israel has to the world. God chose Israel to be the people and nation that would bring forth His Son into the world. After all, He is God and has the right to choose what people and lineage His Son would come from. Through Israel, God would bless the entire world with Jesus who gave Himself as a sacrifice to save the world. This is why the enemy hates Israel and fights against them.

The same promise applies to us individually. As we are a friend to Israel, God will be a friend to us. We can bless Israel in a number of ways.

The number one way is to pray for Israel and the peace of Jerusalem. When we bless Israel, God considers it as though we are blessing Him. Any service done for His people, God will reward. When God is your friend, you don't have enemies.

In Israel all the families of the earth will be blessed. Jesus is the great blessing of the world, the *Treasure of all Treasures*. When we surrender to God's will, we will be most blessed among the inhabitants of the world.

CHAPTER 14

Grieving the Heart of God

Ephesians 4:30

And do not grieve the Holy Spirit of God, by whom you were sealed for the day of redemption.

"Grieve" means, 'to make weary, to sadden, or to pain.' Simply put, we grieve the Spirit of God when we are disobedient and unbelieving. Throughout history the enemy of our soul has been putting fear in the hearts and minds of people about the display or the manifestations of the power and Presence of God. The people of Israel in Exodus were afraid of the Presence of God on Mount Sinai (Exodus 20:18&19). They refused to go near the Lord because of fear. They feared the display of His Presence. Today, in the same way, we have backed away from and pulled back from the One who loves us and gave His life for us because we fear the display of His power and Presence. In Mark 16:17-18, Jesus says these signs will follow those who believe. In His name we will cast out demons, speak with new tongues and heal the sick. This should be a normal way of life for the child of God.

My heart is often heavy about this very thing because so many are missing out on His goodness in their lives because of fear. As the Lord so sweetly does, He spoke to me and said, "My heart is grieved because my people tie my hands when they refuse to cooperate with Me.

Fear has caused My people to pull away therefore they do not cooperate with My Spirit. I have all authority over the enemy and have given it to my people. The enemy is not a problem for Me or My people. The problem is when My people do not cooperate with Me."

Matthew 13:58

Now He did not do many mighty works there because of their unbelief.

I want to make the distinction between doubt and unbelief very clear. Doubt is questioning what we already believe; you can't doubt what you don't believe. Unbelief is a determined refusal to believe. Doubt is a struggle the believer may face. Unbelief is a willful determination not to believe.

Had I known this in my earlier years, it would have alleviated a lot of confusion for me.

Unbelief grieves the heart of God. The Lord did very little miracles in His hometown because of unbelief. Where there is unbelief there is no cooperation with the Spirit of God. It saddens the heart of our Father because He delights in giving us His Kingdom. When He isn't able to do so, He is grieved.

Luke 11:11-13 talks about the goodness of our Father. Our Father wants to do only good by us. If we can trust our earthly fathers to do well by us, how much more can we trust our heavenly Father to do us good? Don't let fear stop you from experiencing the goodness of your Father in heaven.

Let us not grieve the heart of God because of fear, disobedience and unbelief. In spite of the fear you may experience, choose as an act of your will to say, "Yes, Father, not my will but yours." We *cannot* do it without Him; He *will not* do it without us.

CHAPTER 15

Our Worth

One of the names of God is "Yahweh" which means, 'the one who is ever present with His people.' The Lord is present not only in our past and future but He is also present in our **now**. We are to walk with Him daily and trust Him in our **now**; He wants to meet with you **now**.

Like I said earlier, I came from a large family, seventh of ten kids, along with my mom and dad made twelve of us. There were times we would have friends over to live with us for extended periods of time so it felt like our family was larger than what it actually was. Back in the day, large families were very common.

I always felt lost in the shuffle of so many people and circumstances. My dad was a very hard-working man and was away from home often to feed, clothe and house all of us. We all lived in a modest three bedroom home. It was to say the least, a bit crowded. I don't know how my parents did it, but trying to imagine raising so many and keeping my sanity is unthinkable. They did better than I could have done.

With no one to blame and purely because of life circumstances, I have gone through most of my life not feeling valued. I began to look for my worth and value in other people. Of course, when we look for our value and worth from other people, we come up very short and end up feeling more insecure. We can't give what we don't have; neither can we expect other people to give us what only God Himself can give. Not knowing my value and worth caused lots of pain and hurt in my life.

I began to ask the Lord to help me let go of the insecurity because I didn't want to go through life carrying this load. I wanted to be free to live and love as God intended.

The Lord began to show me just how broken I was. It wasn't until He opened my eyes to my brokenness that I began to truly understand the price He paid and just how much I was worth to Him. By learning to live in His Presence, my healing and walk of freedom increased. I realized I couldn't use my past as an excuse for my present bondage and misery. In other words, I had to allow Him to heal the wounds of my past in order to walk in His victory in my present and future. Remember, He is Yahweh, ever-present with us in the *now* to give us victory over the *past* and victory in the *future*.

John 3:16

For God so loved the world that He gave His only begotten Son, that whoever believes in Him should not perish but have everlasting life.

Once we realize the price He paid for our broken lives, then and only then, can He show us our true value. Jesus expressed to us our value when He stretched out His arms on the cross saying, "It is finished." The Father values us as much as He values His own Son. That says something when a father is willing to give his son to die in the place of another. Would you?

Jesus took the cup of the wrath of God upon Himself which should have been ours to bear; in turn He gave us all that He is. If that sounds like an unfair trade, it's because it is. His love isn't fair; it's extravagant and extraordinary. His love is fierce in that He is as fierce as a lion when protecting His cubs and it is extravagant in that He went to the greatest length to save you and me.

Until we know His love for us, we cannot truly love Him, ourselves or others. This is recognized in the first and second commandment in Mark 12:29-31.

Matthew 13: 45 & 46

"Again, the kingdom of heaven is like a merchant looking for fine pearls. When he found one of great value, he went away and sold everything he had and bought it.

Jesus paid a price so high it will take all of eternity to realize just how high and valuable a price He paid. We are only as valuable as the price one is willing to pay. In the world we are valued by what we own, by what we do, and by how much money we have.

Our Father gave His **All** in giving His Son as a ransom for you and me. That's the value He places on us. God values us according to the price He paid for our redemption. As Jesus is valued by the Father, so are we valued. As Jesus is, so are we in this world (1 John 4:17). You and I are the pearl of great value to our Father; His *treasure of all treasures*.

CHAPTER 16

Mirror Mirror

The mirror on the wall has become a common part of our daily lives. So much so, we don't realize just how much it controls us. Many of us, male and female, when looking into the mirror are in a sense asking, as the old fairy tale goes "Mirror, mirror, on the wall, who is the fairest of them all?" We look into the mirror referring to our natural state to obtain our identity. The mirror on the wall can produce a host of negative emotions. It can trigger jealousy, pride, insecurity, competition, etc.

How many times a day do we look into the mirror on the wall? What do we see when we look into the mirror? Whether or not we like what we see, we are more than what we see in the mirror on the wall. If we are seeing through our natural eyes when we look into the mirror, we will be disillusioned and deceived every time. We will see what the world wants us to see; the enemy will blind us and lie to us.

God is the only one who can correct our spiritual sight. It is like putting on a pair of glasses to correct our natural sight. Those glasses help us to see past our natural ability. The Word of God does just that. It helps us to see past our natural ability into spiritual reality.

2 Corinthians 3:18

And all of us, as with unveiled face, as we continue to behold the Word of God as in a mirror the glory of the Lord, are constantly being transfigured into His very own image in ever increasing splendor and from one degree of glory to another: for this comes from the Lord Who is the Spirit.

In James 1:22-25, it states that the Word of God is a mirror. It is the mirror of the glory of God. It is the reflection of Jesus. The Word of God is the reflection of who we truly are as children of God. As we behold the glory of God in the mirror of the Word of God, we are transformed into the same image from glory to glory, line upon line and little by little. The Word (Table of Showbread) and the Spirit (Menorah) work together to transform us into who we were created to be and it corrects our impaired vision to see as God sees.

When we allow the mirror on the wall to dictate to us who we are, we fall far too short of who we were created to be. We must get our identity from the mirror of the Word of God, putting on the Word of God as though we are putting on glasses to correct our sight as we look into the mirror on the wall. We are who He says we are. The mirror of His Word is true, reliable and sharper than a sword, able to divide truth from a lie. It begins to cut away the lies of the world and the enemy and reveals the truth. When our identity is in the mirror of the Word of God, we will look into the mirror on the wall and tell it who we are, not vice versa.

We look into a mirror on the wall to make sure we are presentable; if not, we change what needs to be changed. The mirror of the Word of

God serves the same purpose. You look into it and the Spirit of God begins to show you what needs to be changed and He begins to change you into the image of the Son.

Looking into the mirror of God's Word corrects our vision and gives us a new lens to look through. We begin to see ourselves and the world through the lens or eyes of God.

I have an older sister who has gone on to be with the Lord. She loved the Lord and I have no doubt where she is. She is sitting at the feet of Jesus in worship.

My sister was a very beautiful woman. Later in her life she developed a mental illness and over time that illness began to take its toll on her physically. When she would look into the mirror, I knew it troubled her to see how the illness changed her appearance. One day as I was visiting with her, I felt impressed to tell her that she was more than what she saw in the mirror on the wall.

As I spoke those words to her, her countenance changed. Suddenly, she had a big smile on her face. That word gave her comfort in knowing that she was far more than what she saw in the mirror on the wall. Though her natural beauty was blemished, she began to realize that the Lord saw her very differently. She began to realize she is the beloved of God made in the image of God. Since going on to be with the Lord, she has no more illness and no more pain. She is perfectly beautiful in God's Presence never to be marred by the image in the mirror on the wall again.

Galatians 3:27

For as many of you as were baptized into Christ have put on Christ.

Looking into the mirror of God's Word starts the process of putting on Christ. We become who we were created to be. As Jesus is, so are we in this world.

Today, as I look into the mirror on the wall, I see a new wrinkle here and there. I see a new gray hair here and there. At times, when I look into the mirror, I will hear whispers of what the world and other people say I should be. The Lord quickly reminds me to put on my corrective lens, the Word of God, and I'm reminded that I am more than what I see in the mirror on the wall. I then begin to tell the mirror who I am according to the mirror of God's Word.

He didn't die for the angels or for any other of His creation. He died for you and me. The mirror of the Word of God shouts out to us that we are His treasure of all treasures. Among all of His creation, you and I are who He chose to suffer and die for, to redeem us and to give us abundant life.

CHAPTER 17

The Mandate

In the Tabernacle, the Menorah was to be burning continually, never to go out. God instructed the priest to be careful and watch that the light of the Menorah was always burning, which denotes we are to nurture the Light of the Holy Spirit in our lives so that His Presence burns bright continually. We are to purposefully release the light of His Presence into those we can reach from generation to generation for a perpetual light throughout all eternity.

In the vision the Lord gave to me of the Menorah, I have come to realize He was giving me a mandate. A mandate is an instruction, command or commission. The mandate is to allow the Light of His Presence to continually burn in my heart and to release His Presence to the world around me. This mandate is for all of us. In writing this book, I am fulfilling, in part, the mandate the Lord has given me.

God removed every barrier between us and Himself except our free will. All He requires is a willing and humble heart. I pray that the Father would work in you the will and the ability to do His good pleasure until your greatest joy would be to do the will of your Father.

My desire is to give you a Treasure that moths and rust cannot corrupt, that doesn't fade and will last for eternity. My hope and prayer for you is that you would know the reality of His Presence in your past, present and future. The memory of me will fade, but His Presence is constant and sure from generation to generation, from everlasting to everlasting.

Colossians 1:27

To whom God would make known what is the riches of the glory of this mystery among the Gentiles, which is Christ in you, the hope of glory

Romans 8:19

For the creation waits in eager expectation for the children of God to be revealed.

Jesus in us and revealed through us is the world's hope of glory. How will the world know Him except through His people?

Creation is eagerly waiting for the revealing of the children of God in the power of the Holy Spirit. *Tshalach* to you! May the Lord send forth His Spirit upon you and break out mightily His Spirit in your life. Recognize your time of visitation and do not squander it. Submit to Jesus and let Him in.

Joel 2: 28

"And it shall come to pass afterward that I will pour out My Spirit on all flesh; your sons and your daughters shall prophesy, your old men shall dream dreams, your young men shall see visions. And also on My menservants and on My maidservants I will pour out My Spirit in those days.

To those who are thirsty, come to the Living Waters; to those who are hungry, come to the Bread of life, taste and see that the Lord, He is good.

Just as I have freely received, I freely serve you Jesus, the Bread of Life, and the *Treasure of all Treasures*. He is more precious than silver, more costly than gold and more beautiful than diamonds.

CHAPTER 18

The Blessing

If you are ready to receive this Treasure, pray this prayer and be filled with His Spirit.

Prayer

Father, I believe that Jesus died for my sins. I believe that Jesus was buried and resurrected on the third day. I ask you Father to forgive me of all my sin and wash me with the blood of Jesus. I receive you Jesus as my Lord and Savior. I ask you Jesus to fill me with your Holy Spirit. Baptize me now with your Holy Spirit. I thank you for saving me and filling me with the Holy Spirit.

Blessing Declaration

I declare the Word of the Lord and the Name of God over you:

Isaiah 60:1
Arise, shine; For your light has come! And the glory of the Lord is risen upon you.

Matthew 5:14
You are the light of the world. A city that is set on a hill cannot be hid.

Numbers 6: 24-26
The LORD will bless you and He will keep you. The LORD will make His face to shine upon you and He will be gracious to you.

The LORD will lift His countenance to you and He will establish Shalom for you. And they will put My name upon the children of Israel and I will bless them.